Biometric Spooting

Unmasking the Illusion of Security

Authored by

Zahid Ameer

Published by

Goodword eBooks

DEDICATION

"I dedicate this book to my beloved parents, whose wisdom I hold in the highest regard. Their every word of guidance has been a beacon of light, illuminating the path of my life and shaping the essence of who I am."

Contents:

1. Introduction to Biometrics

In a world increasingly driven by digital transformation and interconnected devices, the need for secure, reliable, and user-friendly authentication mechanisms has never been greater. Traditional methods of authentication—such as passwords, PINs, and tokens—while still prevalent, have proven to be vulnerable to various forms of attack, including phishing, credential stuffing, social engineering, and theft. As a result, there has been a paradigm shift from relying on what you know or what you possess to who you inherently are. This is where **biometrics** comes into play.

What is Biometrics?

The term *biometrics* is derived from the Greek words *bios* (life) and *metron* (measure), literally meaning "life measurement." Biometrics refers to the measurement and statistical analysis of people's unique physical and behavioral characteristics. These characteristics are used to identify and verify individuals.

Biometric authentication systems capture these traits, transform them into digital templates, and compare them against previously stored records for identity verification. These characteristics are difficult to forge, copy, or steal, making them particularly appealing for security applications.

Categories of Biometrics

Biometric identifiers can generally be classified into two broad categories:

8

1. **Physiological Biometrics** – These are physical traits that are genetically determined and relatively stable over time. Examples include:

   - **Fingerprint**

   - **Facial features**

   - **Iris and retina patterns**

   - **Palm veins**

   - **Hand geometry**

   - **DNA**

2. **Behavioral Biometrics** – These are patterns in human activity and behavior that are learned over time and are unique to each individual. Examples include:

   - **Voice**

   - **Typing rhythm**

   - **Gait (the way a person walks)**

   - **Signature dynamics**

   - **Mouse movement or touchscreen interaction**

Each biometric modality comes with its own set of strengths and limitations in terms of uniqueness, permanence, collectability, and resistance to spoofing.

The Rise of Biometrics in Everyday Life

Only a few decades ago, biometric systems were largely the domain of science fiction and high-security government agencies. Today, they are ubiquitous:

- **Smartphones and tablets**: Facial recognition and fingerprint sensors unlock devices and authorize payments.

- **Banking and finance**: Voice recognition and facial ID are used for secure transactions.

- **Airports and border control**: Iris scanning and facial recognition are speeding up the process of identity verification for millions of travelers.

- **Healthcare**: Biometric authentication helps protect sensitive medical records.

- **Workplace security**: Fingerprint and palm scanners ensure that only authorized personnel access certain facilities.

This integration into daily life is driven by the dual promises of **convenience** and **security**. Unlike passwords, biometrics cannot be forgotten, lost, or easily guessed.

Why Biometrics?

Let's look at what makes biometrics so appealing compared to traditional authentication:

- ☑ **Uniqueness**: Every individual has distinctive biometric features.

- ☑ **Non-transferable**: Unlike passwords or cards, biometric traits cannot be shared.

- ☑ **Convenience**: Fast and seamless user experience— just look or touch.

- ☑ **Difficult to forge**: Advanced tech is required to replicate biometric traits.

- ☑ **Increased accountability**: Logs tied to specific individuals reduce fraud and misuse.

However, these advantages come with significant caveats.

The Security Illusion: Are Biometrics Truly Safe?

While biometric authentication may seem more secure on the surface, it introduces a different set of vulnerabilities. The phrase "your body is your password" sounds comforting—until you consider what happens when that password is stolen.

Passwords and PINs can be changed. Biometric data, however, is **permanent**. If someone obtains your fingerprint data or creates a convincing clone of your face, you cannot simply regenerate new biometrics. Moreover, many biometric systems store data in the form of templates—digital representations of traits—which, if compromised, can be reverse-engineered or exploited in spoofing attacks.

Biometric spoofing, a growing concern, involves creating fake biometric samples to trick authentication systems. For example:

- A high-quality photograph can sometimes fool facial recognition.

- Voice synthesis powered by AI can replicate a person's voice.

- Gelatin or 3D-printed fingerprints have bypassed fingerprint sensors.

These developments challenge the notion that biometrics are inherently secure. They also highlight the critical importance of building systems that go beyond simply matching traits to implementing **liveness detection**, **multi-factor authentication**, and **robust encryption**.

The Need for Ethical and Privacy Considerations

Beyond security, biometric authentication raises pressing **privacy and ethical issues**:

- **Consent**: Many biometric systems operate passively, capturing facial images or voice data without explicit permission.

- **Surveillance**: Governments and corporations can use biometrics for mass surveillance, eroding civil liberties.

- **Data storage and misuse**: Once biometric data is stored, there's always a risk of data breaches or unauthorized use.

- **Bias and inaccuracy**: Facial recognition algorithms have shown disparities in accuracy across races and genders, leading to false positives and systemic discrimination.

Regulations like the **General Data Protection Regulation (GDPR)** in the EU and **California Consumer Privacy Act (CCPA)** in the U.S. aim to address some of these concerns, mandating transparency and data protection.

Conclusion: A Double-Edged Sword

Biometrics have transformed the landscape of identity verification. They offer undeniable benefits in speed, convenience, and security. However, they are not a silver bullet. As we move further into a world where our very biology becomes our access key, it is crucial to ensure that these systems are built with foresight, ethical grounding, and security resilience.

The promise of biometrics must be met with **a healthy skepticism** and **continuous innovation** to counteract the threats they also invite. After all, when your identity is your password, you only get one shot at protecting it.

2. What is Biometric Spoofing?

Biometric Spoofing is a form of deception aimed at biometric security systems, where an attacker uses a forged, replicated, or synthetic version of someone's biological traits to gain unauthorized access. Unlike traditional cybersecurity attacks—such as password cracking or phishing—biometric spoofing specifically targets systems that identify individuals based on unique physical or behavioral characteristics like fingerprints, facial features, iris patterns, voice, or even vein structures.

This method of attack is particularly insidious because biometric identifiers are deeply personal and immutable. If your password is compromised, you can change it. If your fingerprint or facial data is compromised, you can't just swap it out for a new one—making the stakes considerably higher.

Why Biometrics?

Biometric authentication has become increasingly popular in recent years for several key reasons:

- **Convenience** – No need to remember complex passwords or carry physical tokens.

- **Speed** – Biometric scans are typically quick and seamless.

15

- **Perceived Security** – Since each person's biometrics are unique, they're considered more secure than knowledge-based credentials.

However, this sense of security is a double-edged sword. Because biometrics are viewed as inherently secure, systems may be less likely to have backup checks or layered protections—making them ripe targets for spoofing.

What Does Spoofing Look Like in Practice?

Biometric spoofing comes in many forms, depending on the biometric modality being targeted. Here's a breakdown:

1. Fingerprint Spoofing

Attackers create replicas of someone's fingerprint using materials like gelatin, silicone, glue, or even 3D-printed molds. They may lift latent prints from surfaces the victim has touched and use them to construct the replica. In many cases, inexpensive tools and publicly available methods are all that's needed to bypass fingerprint scanners.

2. Facial Recognition Spoofing

Simple attacks use high-resolution photographs or printed 2D images of the target's face. More advanced techniques involve video replays or 3D masks that replicate facial features with alarming accuracy. With the rise of deepfake technology, synthetic video representations have also emerged as powerful tools for deception.

3. Iris and Retina Spoofing

These systems are generally considered more secure due to their need for high-resolution imaging. Still, attackers have been known to spoof iris scans using high-quality images printed on paper or contact lenses with embedded iris patterns.

4. Voice Recognition Spoofing

Spoofing in this area can involve using recorded voice samples or leveraging text-to-speech systems to mimic the victim's voice. With AI-powered voice synthesis tools, it's becoming easier than ever to recreate a convincing replica of someone's speech from just a few seconds of recorded audio.

5. Vein Pattern Spoofing

Vein biometrics are harder to spoof because they rely on subdermal patterns, typically detected via near-infrared light. However, researchers have demonstrated that with enough effort and imaging equipment, even these systems can be deceived.

Why is Biometric Spoofing Dangerous?

Irreversible Breach

Unlike a password breach, where credentials can be reset, a biometric breach is *permanent*. You can't grow a new face or change your fingerprints easily.

False Sense of Security

Biometrics are often assumed to be more secure, which may lead to overreliance. In reality, if spoofing techniques evolve faster than detection methods, users are at greater risk than with traditional login systems.

Used in High-Security Areas

Biometrics are frequently employed in sensitive applications:

- **Banking apps and mobile payment systems**

- **Airport and border control**

- **Military and government facilities**

- **Smart home security**

If an attacker spoofs biometric data to gain access in these contexts, the consequences could be severe—from data theft to espionage.

How Spoofing Happens: The Process

1. **Acquisition** – Attacker collects biometric data (e.g., a photo, fingerprint smudge, or audio recording).

2. **Replication** – The data is used to create a synthetic or fake version of the biometric trait.

3. **Presentation** – The replica is presented to the system in an attempt to fool it.

4. **Bypass** – If the spoof is successful, the attacker gains unauthorized access.

This cycle is known in academic literature as a **Presentation Attack (PA)**, and the fake input used is called a **Presentation Attack Instrument (PAI)**.

Targets of Biometric Spoofing

Spoofing isn't just about breaking into someone's phone. Real-world targets include:

- **Smartphones and personal devices** – Face ID, fingerprint scanners.

- **ATMs and banking apps** – Voice authentication and iris scanners.

- **Corporate systems** – Biometric time clocks, secure doors.

- **Airports** – Automated border control gates.

- **Healthcare systems** – Patient authentication and access control.

Tools and Materials Used in Spoofing

- **Molding compounds**: Silicone, gelatin, glue.

- **Printing tech**: High-resolution photo printers, 3D printers.

- **Software**: Deepfake generators, voice synthesizers, AI facial reconstruction tools.

- **Basic items**: Transparent tape, makeup, colored lenses, and even wood glue.

Many spoofing attacks are shockingly low-tech and cheap—raising alarms about widespread vulnerability.

Spoofing vs. Hacking: Key Differences

Factor	Biometric Spoofing	Traditional Hacking
Attack Vector	Physical/Digital (presentation attack)	Software (malware, phishing, brute force)

Target	Biometric authentication system	Network, credentials, databases
Difficulty	Varies from low (photos) to high (3D masks)	Varies (depends on security measures)
Traceability	Often less traceable	More logs and detection mechanisms exist
Permanency of Damage	High (biometrics can't be changed)	Medium (passwords can be reset)

Bottom Line

Biometric spoofing is a potent threat that exposes a major flaw in the very systems we trust most. While biometrics are undeniably convenient and innovative, their vulnerabilities must not be underestimated. As the technology becomes more widespread, the importance of robust anti-spoofing mechanisms, awareness, and layered security grows.

In short, biometric spoofing is not just a tech problem—it's a human security crisis waiting to happen.

3. Types of Biometric Systems

Biometric systems rely on the recognition of unique physiological or behavioral traits for authentication or identification. While they offer a compelling blend of convenience and security, each modality comes with its own set of strengths, weaknesses, and susceptibility to spoofing attacks.

Let's explore the most widely used biometric systems in detail:

---

1. Fingerprint Recognition

Overview

Fingerprint recognition is arguably the most mature and widely used biometric authentication method. It identifies users based on the unique ridges and valleys present on their fingertips. No two fingerprints are exactly alike, making this method both practical and secure for many applications.

Applications

- Mobile devices (smartphones, tablets)

- Access control systems

- Time and attendance tracking

- Criminal investigations (AFIS)

Strengths

- High accuracy and low false acceptance rates

- Compact sensors and low-cost implementation

- Quick processing and user-friendly

Vulnerabilities

Despite its robustness, fingerprint recognition systems can be fooled using:

- **Gummy fingers**: A replica of a fingerprint made from gelatin or other pliable substances.

- **Silicone or latex molds**: Crafted from latent prints or lifted impressions.

- **3D printing**: Scanning a print and creating a solid replica using printing technologies.

Spoofing Case: In 2013, hackers from the Chaos Computer Club successfully spoofed Apple's Touch ID using a lifted fingerprint and a homemade mold, demonstrating the vulnerability of even consumer-grade systems.

2. Facial Recognition

Overview

Facial recognition systems analyze facial features such as the distance between the eyes, nose shape, jawline, and facial contours. With the rise of deep learning and neural networks, facial recognition has become one of the most scalable forms of biometric security.

Applications

- Airport security (e.g., e-passport gates)

- Smartphone unlocking (e.g., Apple Face ID)

- Public surveillance and crowd monitoring

- Payment and banking systems (e.g., Alipay Face Pay)

Strengths

- Non-intrusive and passive

- Can be used in real-time with surveillance feeds

- Easily integrates with existing camera systems

Vulnerabilities

- **Photographic attacks**: Simple photos or high-resolution prints can trick low-grade systems.

- **Video replay attacks**: Looped videos simulate facial movements like blinking.

- **3D mask attacks**: Hyper-realistic masks have been used to fool even sophisticated facial recognition systems.

Spoofing Case: In 2017, Samsung's Galaxy S8 facial recognition feature was tricked with a high-resolution photo displayed on another phone, raising questions about its reliability.

3. Iris Recognition

Overview

Iris recognition analyzes the complex patterns in the colored ring surrounding the pupil. These patterns are stable throughout a person's life and are believed to offer the highest levels of accuracy among physiological biometrics.

Applications

- Border control (e.g., UAE Smart Gates)

- High-security areas (labs, government facilities)

- ATMs and banking

- Healthcare identity verification

Strengths

- Extremely low false match rate (FMR)

- Less affected by aging and environmental conditions

- Difficult to capture without cooperation

Vulnerabilities

- **Printed iris images**: High-resolution iris photos can be used to spoof simpler systems.

- **Synthetic iris patterns**: Generated by software to mimic real iris textures.

- **Contact lenses**: Printed lenses with spoof iris designs have occasionally fooled sensors.

Spoofing Case: In 2012, researchers in Spain used printed images of irises to successfully bypass commercial iris scanners, exposing the risk to high-value security deployments.

---

4. Voice Recognition

Overview

Voice recognition (also known as speaker recognition) identifies individuals based on vocal attributes such as pitch, cadence, accent, tone, and pronunciation patterns. It can be **text-dependent** (using a preset phrase) or **text-independent** (recognizing based on natural speech).

Applications

- Virtual assistants (Siri, Alexa, Google Assistant)

- Telephone banking and customer service

- Secure facility access through voice prompts

- Smart homes and IoT devices

Strengths

- Hands-free and accessible

- Low-cost implementation using microphones

- Can be combined with speech-to-text for multitasking

Vulnerabilities

- **Replay attacks**: Recordings of the user's voice used to gain unauthorized access.

- **Voice synthesis**: AI-generated voices mimicking the target user's vocal patterns.

- **Environmental noise**: Accuracy can degrade with background interference.

Spoofing Case: In 2019, cybercriminals used AI-synthesized voice to impersonate a CEO in a deepfake phone call and tricked a company into transferring over $240,000.

5. Vein Pattern Recognition

Overview

Also called vascular biometrics, vein recognition analyzes the patterns of blood vessels inside a person's hand or finger. Using near-infrared light, the system captures a vein map that is almost impossible to replicate externally.

Applications

- High-security banking and ATMs (e.g., Hitachi VeinID)

- Hospitals and patient ID systems

- Employee authentication in critical infrastructure

Strengths

- Extremely difficult to forge due to internal nature

- Not affected by surface conditions like dirt or cuts

- Contactless or low-contact variants reduce hygiene concerns

Vulnerabilities

- **Infrared imaging**: Some studies have shown that vein patterns can be captured at a distance using specialized IR cameras.

- **Prosthetics or fake hand models**: With inside knowledge and advanced tools, there have been experimental attempts to simulate vein structures.

Spoofing Concern: Although no large-scale attacks have been reported, researchers have demonstrated the theoretical feasibility of spoofing vein systems, urging the need for continuous advancement.

Summary Table: Biometric Modalities at a Glance

Modality	Strengths	Weaknesses / Spoofing Threats

Finger print	Inexpensive, fast, familiar	Molds, gummy fingers, 3D prints
Face	Passive, easy to deploy	Photos, videos, 3D masks
Iris	High accuracy, stable patterns	Printed images, synthetic irises
Voice	Hands-free, easy for remote use	Deepfakes, replay attacks
Vein	Internal pattern, hard to spoof	Infrared image theft, prosthetic simulations

As biometric technology evolves, so too do the techniques designed to undermine it. Understanding each system's vulnerabilities is critical not only for developers and security professionals, but for everyday users whose privacy and data may be at stake.

4. Techniques of Spoofing for Each Modality

Biometric spoofing techniques have become increasingly sophisticated with advancements in technology, material sciences, and artificial intelligence. Below is a comprehensive exploration of spoofing techniques used to deceive various biometric authentication systems.

Fingerprint Spoofing

Fingerprint recognition is one of the oldest and most widespread biometric technologies, making it a prime target for spoofing. Two major techniques dominate this attack vector:

Molds from Latent Prints Using Gelatin, Silicone, or Glue

Attackers can create a fake fingerprint from **latent prints**—the residues left on surfaces like glasses, phones, or door handles. Here's how it works:

- **Step 1: Lifting the Print** – A latent print is made visible using powder or specialized scanning techniques.

- **Step 2: Capturing the Ridge Pattern** – The print is photographed or scanned to extract the fingerprint pattern.

- **Step 3: Creating the Mold** – The pattern is etched into a surface (like wax or resin), then a mold is cast using substances such as:

    - **Gelatin** (common in gummy bears)

    - **Silicone** (used in prosthetics)

    - **Glue** (like wood glue or epoxy)

These fake fingerprints can fool scanners that lack liveness detection, especially older capacitive or optical sensors.

3D-Printed Replicas from Digital Data

With access to digital fingerprint data (via stolen records, medical imaging, or sensor breaches), attackers can:

- Use **CAD software** to model the ridge structures.

- Employ **3D printers** to create high-fidelity replicas using flexible polymers.

- Apply skin-like materials to enhance realism.

This method requires more technical skill but can bypass high-resolution scanners if done precisely.

Face Spoofing

Facial recognition systems are widely adopted due to their contactless convenience—but they are surprisingly vulnerable to creative spoofing techniques.

Static Image Attacks: Printed Photos

One of the simplest methods:

- A high-resolution photograph of the target is printed.

- When shown to a camera-based face recognition system, it may be accepted as legitimate—especially if the system doesn't require depth perception.

Cheap systems without depth or motion analysis are especially vulnerable.

Video Replay Attacks: Looped Videos Showing Eye Blinking

A more advanced attack using:

- A **short video clip** of the person blinking, turning their head, or smiling.

- Played back on a screen or tablet in front of the sensor.

This can fool systems that rely on minimal motion cues to determine liveness.

Mask Attacks: Hyper-Realistic 3D Masks

The most sophisticated form of face spoofing involves:

- **3D-printing or sculpting** a face using photos and depth data.

- Materials like **latex**, **silicone**, or **resin** can be painted and textured to resemble real skin.

- These masks even simulate contours, shadows, and reflections of real faces.

Such attacks can fool systems without strong liveness or infrared checks, as demonstrated in high-profile security demonstrations.

Iris Spoofing

Iris recognition is considered highly secure due to the uniqueness and complexity of the iris pattern. However, two notable spoofing techniques have emerged:

Printed Iris Images on Contact Lenses

- The attacker prints the target's iris pattern using a high-resolution image.

- The image is transferred onto a **custom contact lens**.

- The lens is worn or applied to a dummy eye to present to the scanner.

This method can deceive systems that fail to verify natural eye reflectivity, dilation, or blood vessels.

Synthetic Iris Generation Through Image Processing

Using image processing software:

- Fake irises are created that resemble real patterns but are generated from scratch or altered from other images.

- These images are then displayed on screens or printed and presented to sensors.

- Attackers may manipulate contrast, lighting, and pupil dilation effects to simulate a real iris.

Advanced AI tools can even create "synthetic identities" with no real-world counterpart—an emerging concern.

Voice Spoofing

Voice recognition systems are increasingly integrated into banking, customer service, and IoT devices. However, they are highly susceptible to audio manipulation.

Replay Attacks Using Recordings

- A voice sample of the target (often from phone calls, YouTube videos, or podcasts) is recorded.

- Specific phrases or commands are replayed to the system.

- If the voiceprint and timing match, access may be granted.

This method is simple but effective, especially if the system does not analyze background noise, tone consistency, or audio source characteristics.

AI Voice Cloning to Synthesize New Phrases

The most advanced threat in voice spoofing comes from **AI-generated voices**:

- Tools like **Lyrebird**, **Descript**, or **ElevenLabs** can clone a voice using only a few minutes of audio.

- Attackers can then synthesize **custom commands** or conversations in the target's voice.

- These voices can be eerily accurate in terms of tone, rhythm, and emotion.

If the biometric system lacks detection for artifacts, pitch irregularities, or synthesized waveforms, it may fall prey to such attacks.

Vein Spoofing

Vein recognition is harder to spoof because it captures subdermal patterns using near-infrared light. Still, researchers and attackers have found potential methods:

Infrared Imaging to Capture Patterns

- Infrared cameras can be used to photograph someone's vein structure from a distance, such as:

  - Through glass

  - From security footage

- These patterns are extracted and processed into templates.

Although this requires access to specialized imaging tools, once obtained, it forms the basis for a physical replica.

Printed or Prosthetic Veins Simulated for Bypass

Using the captured vein patterns:

- A **prosthetic hand** with printed vein lines using **conductive ink** or **IR-absorbing material** is created.

- Alternatively, patterns are printed onto a flat surface and heated to simulate blood flow.

- When presented to a vein scanner, it may read the pattern as legitimate.

Because veins are deeper than fingerprints, spoofing is more complex, but not impossible—especially as 3D printing and imaging improve.

Conclusion: Why These Techniques Matter

Biometric spoofing isn't just science fiction—it's a real and evolving threat. Each technique exploits a unique vulnerability in how systems read and verify human traits. As spoofing tools become more accessible and AI-generated fakes improve, the need for **liveness detection**, **multimodal systems**, and **behavioral analysis** grows stronger.

Understanding these spoofing techniques is the first step toward building more robust defenses and safeguarding biometric security in the modern age.

5. Real-World Examples of Spoofing Attacks

As biometric systems gained popularity for their promise of secure and seamless authentication, they also became attractive targets for attackers seeking to exploit their vulnerabilities. Though biometrics are often perceived as unbreakable due to their reliance on unique human characteristics, the following real-world incidents prove that even the most advanced systems can be deceived.

1. CCC Hack (2013): A Fingerprint Recreated from Photos

One of the most widely cited cases of biometric spoofing occurred in **December 2013**, when **Jan Krissler**, also known by his hacker alias "**Starbug**," shocked the cybersecurity world at the **Chaos Communication Congress (CCC)** in Hamburg, Germany.

What Happened?

Krissler claimed that he had successfully **reconstructed the fingerprint** of then-German Defense Minister **Ursula von der Leyen** using nothing more than **high-resolution photographs** of her hand.

How Did He Do It?

- During a press conference, journalists captured close-up shots of von der Leyen as she gestured.

- Krissler used a **standard digital camera** and zoomed in on her **right thumbprint** from multiple angles.

- With **commercial fingerprint reconstruction software**, he processed the images and created a **digital replica**.

- He then printed the fingerprint onto a transparent sheet using **latex or wood glue**, materials often used in spoofing.

Implications

This attack was groundbreaking because:

- It **didn't require physical contact** with the target.

- It **exploited public imagery**—available to anyone.

- It revealed that **fingerprints left on glasses, doorknobs, or even photographs** could be harvested and used maliciously.

Krissler warned that world leaders and public figures should **avoid waving their hands** or having high-res photos taken if they rely on biometric security—an ironic but serious piece of advice in the digital age.

2. Samsung Galaxy S8 Face Unlock (2017): Foiled by a Photo

When Samsung released the **Galaxy S8** in 2017, it was marketed as having advanced **facial recognition** capable of unlocking the phone faster than ever before. However, security researchers and hobbyists quickly discovered that the system was far from foolproof.

What Happened?

A group of researchers from **Chaos Computer Club (CCC)—** again!—demonstrated that the S8's face recognition could be **easily tricked with a printed photo** of the phone's owner.

How Did They Do It?

- They printed a **high-resolution photo** of the phone owner's face.

- The photo was **cropped and adjusted** to match the real-world size and proportions.

- Holding the photo in front of the phone's front camera **bypassed the facial recognition lock** and granted access.

Implications

- The exploit exposed a **critical flaw** in Samsung's implementation of facial recognition.

- The system **lacked liveness detection**, such as eye movement, depth perception, or infrared verification.

- It highlighted the **overreliance on convenience** over security in commercial biometrics.

Samsung responded by recommending users switch to more secure options like **iris scanning** or **PINs**—but the damage to public confidence was already done.

---

3. Deepfake Voices (2020s): Synthetic Speech for Social Engineering

As AI advanced in the 2020s, **deepfake technology**—particularly synthetic voices—began to emerge as one of the most insidious tools for biometric spoofing. These voices are generated using **AI models trained on samples of a person's speech**, allowing machines to replicate their tone, cadence, and emotion with eerie accuracy.

Real-World Case: UK-Based Energy Firm Scammed

In **2019**, a deepfake voice was used to successfully defraud a **UK-based energy firm**, marking one of the **first publicly confirmed corporate scams** using synthetic audio.

How Did It Happen?

- The company's CEO received a phone call from someone who sounded exactly like the **German CEO of**

their parent company.

- The voice instructed the UK CEO to **transfer €220,000 (around $243,000)** to a Hungarian supplier urgently.

- Believing the request to be legitimate, the funds were transferred without hesitation.

It was later discovered that the voice was **AI-generated** using samples likely sourced from public speeches and interviews.

Implications

- **Voice biometrics**—once considered secure due to vocal uniqueness—are now vulnerable to **deepfake manipulation**.

- This event demonstrated that **biometrics alone are no longer enough** for authentication, especially when used in high-stakes scenarios.

- It underscored the need for **multi-factor authentication** and **behavioral analysis** to identify inconsistencies beyond voice.

Lessons Learned

These cases each serve as powerful reminders that **biometric systems are not impervious** to attack:

1. **Accessibility of biometric data**—such as faces and voices—makes it inherently more vulnerable than passwords.

2. **Sophisticated spoofing techniques** are no longer the domain of advanced hackers; many can be carried out with **readily available tools and software**.

3. **Trust in biometric systems** should be tempered with an understanding of their limitations—and the inclusion of **additional security layers** is essential.

Final Thought

The illusion of security created by biometrics can be dangerously misleading. These real-world examples illustrate that the key to robust security isn't in eliminating all vulnerabilities—but in **acknowledging them**, **understanding the risks**, and **building smarter systems** that anticipate deception.

In the arms race between attackers and defenders, knowledge is the most powerful biometric of all.

6. The Science of Liveness Detection

As biometric systems become increasingly integrated into daily life—from unlocking phones to accessing bank accounts—their vulnerability to spoofing attacks grows. Simple photos, silicone fingerprints, or AI-generated voices can potentially bypass these systems. To combat such threats, researchers and developers have turned to an advanced defense strategy: **liveness detection**.

Liveness detection focuses on one crucial question: **"Is this biometric trait coming from a real, living person?"**

This isn't just a matter of recognizing a face or a fingerprint; it's about ensuring the biological signs of life are present. Let's dive deep into the science behind liveness detection and the innovative techniques employed to distinguish real from fake.

What Is Liveness Detection?

Liveness detection is a **biometric security feature** designed to assess whether the biometric sample presented to a sensor or system originates from a living individual rather than a static artifact, a recording, or a digitally synthesized model.

There are **two primary categories** of liveness detection:

- **Active Liveness Detection**: Requires user cooperation (e.g., blink, smile, turn head).

- **Passive Liveness Detection**: Detects life signs automatically without user awareness or interaction.

The sophistication of liveness detection varies depending on the biometric modality (e.g., face, fingerprint, voice), but the goal is always the same: prevent spoofing.

Key Techniques in Liveness Detection

Let's explore the various biological and behavioral indicators used in modern systems:

---

1. Eye Blinking Detection

Why It Works: Blinking is a spontaneous, involuntary action that is hard to replicate convincingly in photos, videos, or masks.

Application:

- Facial recognition systems often prompt the user to blink or detect natural blinking as a passive test.

- Some systems track **blink rate and irregularities**, which differ between live faces and pre-recorded footage.

Spoof Resistance:

- A printed image or static photo cannot blink.

- Video attacks must simulate realistic blinking, but subtle discrepancies in timing or smoothness can be detected by AI algorithms.

---

2. Facial Micro-Expressions

Why It Works: Micro-expressions are brief, involuntary facial movements that reflect genuine emotions and reactions.

Application:

- Systems analyze these tiny muscle movements—such as eyebrow twitches, slight lip curls, or eye crinkles—that occur within milliseconds.

- Advanced facial recognition integrates **emotion recognition** as part of liveness detection.

Spoof Resistance:

- Hard to fake with still images or 3D masks.

- Even deepfake videos struggle to produce consistent, involuntary micro-expressions in real time.

---

3. Pulse Detection (Photoplethysmography - PPG)

Why It Works: Blood flow causes tiny color changes in the skin that can be captured with camera sensors.

Application:

- Systems use **optical sensors** or **RGB/IR cameras** to detect **pulse-induced skin tone fluctuations**, typically in the face or fingertips.

- Some smartphones use near-infrared light to monitor these subtle changes.

Spoof Resistance:

- A photo or mask doesn't have blood flow.

- Even high-quality 3D replicas lack pulsation rhythms.

Advantage:

- Non-intrusive and passive, offering continuous liveness monitoring.

4. Skin Elasticity and Texture Analysis

Why It Works: Human skin exhibits natural elasticity and micro-level textures that are hard to mimic.

Application:

- Fingerprint scanners use **capacitive sensing** to measure the electrical properties of skin.

- 3D facial recognition systems assess **depth, contour, and texture** to determine if the face is organic.

- Some systems test for **moisture levels, subdermal ridges, or deformation behavior** when pressed.

Spoof Resistance:

- Fake fingerprints made of gelatin, glue, or silicone may fool simpler sensors, but not advanced ones that test skin response to pressure or heat.

5. Thermal Imaging

Why It Works: Living bodies emit infrared radiation (heat), creating a distinct thermal signature.

Application:

- **Thermal cameras** capture heat maps of the face or hands.

- **Face recognition systems** may compare visible and thermal images for inconsistencies.

Spoof Resistance:

- Printed images and masks do not emit heat patterns.

- Even if heated artificially, fake objects fail to reproduce accurate thermal distributions of a live human.

Works even in darkness or variable lighting.

---

6. Voice Inflection and Frequency Variation

Why It Works: A live human voice has natural variations in tone, pitch, volume, and rhythm that are difficult to replicate accurately.

Application:

- Voice recognition systems analyze **intonation patterns, speech dynamics, background noise**, and **breath patterns**.

- They also track **live interaction cues**, such as call-and-response behavior.

Spoof Resistance:

- Pre-recorded or AI-generated voices often lack the spontaneity and natural variance of real speech.

- Deepfake voice models may be caught by analyzing artifacts and inconsistencies in frequency modulation or timing.

Advanced Technologies Supporting Liveness Detection

To make these techniques effective, biometric systems often employ a blend of **hardware and software**:

- **Infrared & 3D Sensors**: Provide depth data and heat profiles.

- **Machine Learning Algorithms**: Trained to recognize patterns of live versus spoof inputs.

- **Neural Networks & GAN Detection**: Used to detect synthetic inputs created by generative adversarial networks.

- **Sensor Fusion**: Combining data from multiple sources (e.g., video + thermal + depth) for more robust analysis.

Challenges and Limitations

Despite its promise, liveness detection faces several challenges:

- **False Rejections**: Legitimate users may be denied access due to poor lighting, illness, or device limitations.

- **Privacy Concerns**: Some liveness methods, like thermal imaging or continuous monitoring, raise ethical and data protection issues.

- **Adaptive Spoofing**: Attackers evolve—using heated masks, animated deepfakes, or responsive AI-generated voices to bypass systems.

Conclusion: A Living Shield

Liveness detection transforms biometric authentication from mere pattern recognition to dynamic, real-time verification of life. By harnessing involuntary human traits—like a pulse, a blink, or a spontaneous twitch—it forms a powerful barrier against spoofing attempts.

As biometric spoofing methods grow more sophisticated, so too must our defenses. The future of liveness detection lies in

multimodal systems, **AI-powered analysis**, and a seamless integration of **biometric and behavioral** markers. It's a race of evolution—between the ingenuity of attackers and the resilience of technology.

7. AI and Biometric Spoofing

The Double-Edged Sword of Artificial Intelligence

Artificial Intelligence (AI) has transformed the landscape of biometric security. It has enhanced the accuracy of facial recognition, streamlined identity verification processes, and improved the sophistication of anti-spoofing techniques. Yet, paradoxically, the very tools that bolster biometric defenses also equip attackers with the power to breach them. This paradox lies at the heart of biometric spoofing in the age of AI.

A Dual-Use Technology

AI is a **dual-use technology**—it can be used for both defense and offense. While companies and governments integrate AI into biometric systems to detect fraudulent attempts and increase precision, cybercriminals, hackers, and fraudsters are using the same advancements to break through these systems using sophisticated spoofing techniques.

Generative Adversarial Networks (GANs): The Engine Behind Spoof Creation

One of the most disruptive AI technologies in this arena is **Generative Adversarial Networks (GANs)**. Introduced by Ian Goodfellow in 2014, GANs consist of two neural networks:

- A **generator**, which creates fake data.

- A **discriminator**, which evaluates data and distinguishes between real and fake.

These two networks compete in a kind of technological cat-and-mouse game, ultimately refining the fake outputs until they become nearly indistinguishable from genuine samples.

How GANs Enable Spoofing:

- **Facial Spoofing**: GANs can generate photorealistic facial images of individuals who may not even exist. These can be used to bypass facial recognition systems that lack liveness detection.

- **Fingerprint Replication**: GANs trained on fingerprint datasets can synthesize fingerprints capable of matching with real user profiles in low-quality or poorly defended systems.

- **Iris and Retina Cloning**: By feeding thousands of high-resolution iris scans into a GAN, an attacker can synthesize synthetic irises that mimic the statistical patterns of legitimate users.

GANs don't just replicate real individuals—they can also create "master biometric" templates that match a wide range of identities. This was demonstrated in research where AI-generated "master fingerprints" could match up to 20% of identities in certain datasets, posing a huge security risk.

Deepfakes: Real-Time Mimicry of Human Traits

Perhaps the most publicly recognized face of AI-driven spoofing is the **deepfake**—synthetic media in which a person's likeness is replaced with someone else's using deep learning.

Real-Time Facial Deepfakes

Deepfake technology has evolved from offline image synthesis to real-time video generation. Tools like DeepFaceLab and FaceSwap allow attackers to:

- **Mimic facial expressions**, including blinking, smiling, and speaking.

- **Superimpose faces** on live video feeds.

- **Bypass facial recognition systems** with convincing animated loops.

This means someone could potentially attend a video-based ID verification session while using another person's digital face, complete with realistic movements and expressions.

AI-Generated Voice Cloning

Voice deepfakes are equally alarming. AI tools such as Descript's Overdub, Resemble.ai, and ElevenLabs can replicate someone's voice using just a few minutes of audio. With enough data, attackers can:

- Simulate speech in real-time.

- Respond to voice-based authentication prompts.

- Fool smart assistants, phone banking systems, and even biometric locks that rely on voice commands.

In one high-profile case, fraudsters used AI-generated audio of a CEO's voice to trick a subordinate into transferring $243,000 to a fake account—a striking demonstration of how deepfake voices can be weaponized.

Irony in Action: AI Defending Against AI

The irony lies in the fact that **AI is also the most promising defense** against these attacks. Just as GANs and deepfakes challenge biometric integrity, AI-powered anti-spoofing mechanisms are being developed to counter them. This includes:

- **Adversarial Training**: Exposing biometric systems to known spoofing attempts during training so they learn to recognize and reject them.

- **Liveness Detection via AI**: Advanced computer vision and audio analysis can detect subtle signs of fakeness, such as unnatural blinking patterns, pixel-level anomalies, or voice frequency inconsistencies.

- **Multi-modal AI Verification**: Combining multiple biometric inputs (e.g., face + voice + fingerprint) and having an AI analyze the interplay between them increases security.

However, there's a **cat-and-mouse dynamic** at play: as defenses get smarter, so do the attackers. It's an ongoing arms race, with each side adapting to the other's improvements.

Emerging Concerns and Challenges

Data Poisoning

Attackers can feed corrupted data into AI systems during their learning phase (especially in open-source environments), causing the model to learn incorrect patterns—essentially teaching it how to be spoofed.

Synthetic Identity Theft

By merging real and fake biometric traits, attackers can create "synthetic identities" that don't exist but are verifiable by current systems—making fraud harder to detect.

Zero-Day Spoofs

As AI-generated content becomes more sophisticated, even the best systems might not catch a new, previously unseen attack pattern—referred to as a zero-day biometric spoof.

Looking Ahead: Redefining Trust in Biometric Systems

As AI becomes increasingly integrated into our biometric infrastructure, a deeper question emerges: *How do we define identity and trust when even the most personal traits can be digitally forged?*

To move forward, the security community must:

- **Standardize anti-spoofing benchmarks** and protocols globally.

- **Adopt AI transparency**, ensuring systems can explain why access was granted or denied.

- **Educate the public and industries** about both the power and peril of AI in biometrics.

Final Thoughts

The relationship between AI and biometric spoofing is paradoxical but unavoidable. On one hand, AI is the defender—

an intelligent gatekeeper. On the other, it is the forger—an illusionist capable of imitating life. In this evolving arena, security is not a fixed goal but a moving target, and understanding both the threat and the solution is key to staying one step ahead.

The future will not be decided by technology alone, but by how wisely and ethically we wield it.

8. Countermeasures and Anti-Spoofing Technologies

Biometric systems are attractive because of their speed and convenience—but with that convenience comes a significant risk: **spoofing**. To mitigate these risks, advanced **countermeasures** have been developed, categorized into three primary layers:

1. **Hardware-Based Technologies**

2. **Software-Based Defenses**

3. **Policy-Based Strategies**

Each of these plays a vital role in building a robust and resilient biometric security framework.

Hardware-Based Countermeasures

These rely on **physical devices or sensors** embedded in biometric systems to detect signs of spoofing or liveness.

Infrared Sensors

Function: Infrared (IR) sensors detect **heat signatures, blood flow**, or **infrared reflectivity** in a presented biometric sample (e.g., face or hand).

Use Cases:

- **Facial Recognition**: IR cameras capture depth and heat to distinguish between a live face and a flat photo.

- **Vein Recognition**: Detects the unique pattern of veins beneath the skin by how blood absorbs IR light.

- **Iris Scanning**: IR illumination enhances iris detail while detecting blinking or natural eye movement.

Spoof Protection:

- Fake faces (e.g., photos or videos) lack the appropriate heat signature.

- IR can detect cold silicone fingerprints that don't emit body heat.

- Dynamic blood flow and thermal changes can confirm "liveness."

Limitations:

- IR sensors increase cost and power consumption.

- Environmental heat or extremely cold surroundings may affect accuracy.

Depth-Sensing Cameras

Function: These cameras measure the **distance between objects** and create a **3D map** of the biometric subject, such as a face or fingerprint.

Technologies:

- **Structured Light** (e.g., Apple's Face ID): Projects a pattern of light and measures distortion.

- **Time-of-Flight (ToF) Cameras**: Calculate the time it takes for light to bounce back.

Spoof Protection:

- A 2D photograph lacks depth; a depth sensor can instantly flag it.

- Videos or replay attacks don't exhibit the proper depth dynamics.

- Advanced spoofing with 3D masks is still detectable via micro-depth inconsistencies.

Limitations:

- Vulnerable to well-made high-resolution 3D printed masks.

- Can be expensive and add bulk to compact systems.

Heartbeat Sensors

Function: Detect **cardiac pulse**, **blood oxygen level**, or **electrocardiographic patterns (ECG)** as a proof of liveness.

Use Cases:

- Integrated into smartwatches, fingerprint scanners, or even palm scanners.

- ECG-based authentication uses electrical signals from the heart that are **unique per person**.

Spoof Protection:

- A fake hand or fingerprint mold won't have a pulse.

- Cannot replicate individual heartbeat variability or rhythm.

- Especially useful in preventing spoofing via prosthetics or physical replicas.

Limitations:

- Intrusive for quick authentication tasks.

- Requires continuous or direct skin contact.

Software-Based Countermeasures

Software solutions use intelligent algorithms, machine learning, and behavior analysis to detect anomalies and signs of spoofing.

Behavioral Biometrics

Function: Analyzes **how** a user interacts with a device rather than **what** they present.

Examples:

- **Keystroke dynamics**: Timing, speed, and rhythm while typing.

- **Mouse movement, touchscreen pressure, swipe gestures**, and **scroll patterns**.

- **Gait analysis** using accelerometers.

Spoof Protection:

- Hard to replicate subtle, involuntary behaviors.

- Can be used passively in the background without user interaction.

- Continual authentication ensures a hijacker is caught mid-session.

Limitations:

- Requires lots of behavioral data for accuracy.

- May struggle with changes in behavior due to stress or injury.

AI-Powered Spoof Detection

Function: Machine learning models trained on real vs fake biometric samples detect minute discrepancies using image analysis, heat maps, or voice pattern shifts.

Use Cases:

- **Facial recognition systems** can detect unnatural skin textures or blink rates.

- **Voice verification** tools can recognize synthesized or replayed voices.

- AI identifies tiny inconsistencies humans can't see—like how light reflects differently on real skin vs a photo.

Spoof Protection:

- Adapts over time and learns from new threats.

- Can respond to novel spoofing methods using anomaly detection.

Limitations:

- Requires a lot of training data.

- Vulnerable to adversarial attacks that "fool" the AI.

Multimodal Authentication

Function: Combines two or more biometric modalities, such as:

- Face + voice

- Fingerprint + iris

- Behavior + facial recognition

Spoof Protection:

- Even if one trait is spoofed, the attacker must also spoof the second (or third) modality.

- Increases complexity and lowers the chance of false positives.

- Highly resilient against single-mode spoofing attacks.

Limitations:

- Requires more hardware/sensors.

- May affect user experience and speed.

Policy-Based Countermeasures

These are **organizational or system-level policies** that enhance security by governing how and when biometric authentication is used.

Risk-Based Authentication

Function: Adapts the **level of security required** based on **contextual factors**, such as:

- Unusual location

- New device login

- Accessing sensitive data

- Abnormal time of day

Examples:

- If logging in from a foreign country, ask for secondary biometric verification.

- If the user's behavior deviates from normal (e.g., typing speed), trigger step-up authentication.

Spoof Protection:

- Reduces attack success by increasing scrutiny only when something seems "off."

- Ensures low-friction user experience under normal conditions but blocks high-risk access.

Limitations:

- May frustrate users during legitimate travel or activity changes.

- Requires robust analytics and user baselines.

Periodic Re-enrollment

Function: Requires users to periodically update their biometric data and verify identity afresh.

Purpose:

- Accounts for physical changes over time (e.g., facial aging, voice tone shifts).

- Removes old, potentially compromised templates.

- Keeps system datasets clean and current.

Spoof Protection:

- Prevents long-term spoofing from outdated or stolen data.

- Increases the likelihood of detecting impersonation during re-verification.

Limitations:

- Can be inconvenient or overlooked by users.

- Needs secure storage and data handling during the re-enrollment process.

Final Thoughts on Anti-Spoofing Measures

Combating biometric spoofing requires a **multi-layered defense approach**. No single countermeasure is foolproof— but combining:

- **Advanced sensors,**

- **AI and behavioral models**, and

- **Smart authentication policies**

can significantly reduce the risk of unauthorized access. The key is to balance **security**, **user experience**, and **privacy**— creating systems that are not only hard to fool but also easy to use.

9. Ethical and Privacy Implications

Biometric authentication is increasingly becoming embedded in the fabric of modern life. From unlocking smartphones and verifying banking transactions to controlling access to buildings and monitoring individuals in public spaces, biometric systems promise seamless security. However, this convenience comes with serious **ethical and privacy risks**, especially when these systems are misused or compromised.

The cornerstone issue? **Biometrics are biologically tied to us—** and unlike passwords or credit cards, they cannot be changed if stolen. This permanence makes the ethical considerations surrounding biometric collection, storage, and usage critically important.

---

1. Data Misuse: When Biological Identity Becomes a Commodity

Biometric data—like fingerprints, iris scans, facial patterns, and voiceprints—are among the most personal data that can be collected from individuals. However, in the digital age, data is power, and power often leads to exploitation.

Risks:

- **Commercial exploitation**: Biometric data can be sold or shared without user consent, particularly by third-party vendors or data brokers. Some companies aggregate facial recognition data to build massive training sets used in AI and surveillance applications.

- **Data breaches**: Unlike passwords that can be reset, stolen biometrics are irrevocable. For example, in 2015, the U.S. Office of Personnel Management (OPM) breach exposed the fingerprints of over 5.6 million federal employees.

- **Profiling and discrimination**: Biometric data may be used to categorize individuals based on race, gender, or health characteristics—leading to biased treatment or denial of services.

Case Example:

- In 2020, **Clearview AI** scraped billions of facial images from the internet, including social media platforms, to build a facial recognition tool without user consent. This led to backlash and multiple lawsuits over privacy violations.

---

2. Surveillance: The Dystopian Edge of Biometrics

Biometric technologies are increasingly used by **governments and corporations for surveillance**, raising significant civil liberty concerns.

Government Surveillance:

- **Mass facial recognition** is deployed in cities and transit hubs to monitor citizens in real-time. This creates a "digital panopticon," where individuals are constantly watched—often without their knowledge.

- **Predictive policing tools** integrate facial data with crime analytics, raising concerns about reinforcing racial and socio-economic biases.

Corporate Surveillance:

- **Employee tracking** using fingerprint scanners or facial recognition at workplaces may infringe on worker privacy.

- **Customer behavior monitoring** in retail environments through cameras and AI-based emotion detection may cross ethical boundaries.

The Ethical Dilemma:

Surveillance might enhance security, but it also threatens **anonymity, freedom of movement, and freedom of expression**. The more we normalize being watched, the more we erode the foundation of a free society.

---

3. Consent: The Illusion of Choice in Biometric Collection

In many contexts, biometric data is collected **passively and non-consensually**—especially facial recognition in public spaces. This challenges the basic principle of **informed consent**, a pillar of ethical data collection.

Issues:

- **Passive scanning**: Cameras in public places may analyze facial features without individuals realizing they're being scanned.

- **Coercion or lack of alternatives**: Many systems offer no non-biometric alternative. For example, if a workplace mandates fingerprint scans for time-tracking, employees may feel forced to give up their biometric data.

- **Children and vulnerable populations**: The use of biometrics in schools or by law enforcement on minors raises serious ethical questions about autonomy and long-term consequences.

Example:

- In the UK, some schools have used fingerprint scanners to manage lunch payments—often without full parental consent. Privacy advocates warn that this normalizes biometric tracking from an early age.

4. Legal Protections: GDPR, CCPA, and Beyond

Recognizing the sensitivity of biometric data, several legal frameworks are beginning to address the need for stronger protections.

GDPR (General Data Protection Regulation) – Europe

- Classifies biometric data as "sensitive personal data."

- Requires **explicit consent** before collection or processing.

- Mandates **data minimization**—only collecting what is necessary.

- Enforces the **right to erasure**, meaning users can request deletion of their biometric data.

- Imposes heavy fines for non-compliance.

CCPA (California Consumer Privacy Act) – United States

- Gives California residents the right to know what personal data is collected and how it's used.

- Grants the ability to **opt out of the sale of personal data**.

- Recognizes biometric data under personal information, though protections aren't as stringent as GDPR.

Other Legal Efforts:

- **Illinois BIPA (Biometric Information Privacy Act)** is one of the strictest state laws in the U.S., requiring **informed written consent** and providing the right to sue for violations.

- Globally, countries like Canada, Australia, Brazil, and India are developing or revising privacy legislation to incorporate biometric protections.

The Need for Ethical Frameworks

While legal protections are essential, they must be complemented by **ethical frameworks** that prioritize human dignity, autonomy, and transparency. Key principles should include:

- **Informed Consent**: Transparent, understandable policies must be in place.

- **Purpose Limitation**: Use biometric data only for the purpose it was collected.

- **Data Minimization**: Avoid collecting excessive or unnecessary data.

- **Non-Discrimination**: Systems must be tested to avoid racial, gender, or age-based biases.

- **Accountability and Redress**: Users should have clear ways to report misuse and demand action.

Conclusion: Privacy at the Crossroads

As biometric technology continues to permeate everyday life, society stands at a crossroads. We must choose between embracing innovation blindly—or demanding that it serves humanity without compromising privacy, freedom, or trust.

The ethical implications of biometric spoofing and misuse are not mere hypotheticals. They are real, present, and rapidly evolving. By recognizing these challenges and pushing for robust ethical and legal safeguards, we can ensure a future where biometrics enhance security **without making us prisoners of our own biology.**

10. The Future of Biometric Security

As our world becomes increasingly interconnected, the demand for seamless, secure, and user-friendly authentication methods continues to grow. Biometric technologies have risen to prominence for their convenience and ability to tie digital identities directly to unique physical or behavioral traits. However, the vulnerabilities exposed by biometric spoofing, deepfakes, and AI-generated attacks signal an urgent need to evolve beyond traditional biometric paradigms.

The future of biometric security lies not in abandoning biometrics, but in **innovating, augmenting, and integrating** them with cutting-edge technologies. Let's explore four emerging frontiers that are poised to revolutionize biometric security:

---

1. Behavioral Biometrics: The Rhythm of Being You

Unlike traditional biometrics, which focus on static features (e.g., your fingerprint or face), **behavioral biometrics** capture **dynamic, ongoing patterns** in human behavior. These systems analyze how you interact with devices and digital environments—essentially, how you "live" online.

Key Behavioral Traits:

- **Gait Analysis**: The way you walk is as unique as your fingerprint. Motion sensors in smartwatches and smartphones can map gait patterns to verify identity in real time.

- **Typing Rhythm**: Known as *keystroke dynamics*, this involves analyzing how quickly and consistently you press keys, dwell times, and latency between strokes.

- **Mouse & Screen Interaction**: The path your cursor takes, scrolling behavior, pressure sensitivity, and even screen swipe patterns (on mobile) can uniquely identify you.

- **Voice Cadence & Inflection**: While voiceprint alone can be spoofed, combining it with emotional tone and speech timing adds resilience against impersonation.

Advantages:

- **Passive and continuous** authentication.

- **Difficult to spoof** since it involves subconscious behavior.

- **No need for user intervention**, making it seamless.

Challenges:

- Requires large datasets to build accurate models.

- Can be affected by stress, illness, or injury.

- Raises concerns about constant surveillance and privacy.

---

2. Brainwave Authentication: The Mind as the Key

Imagine unlocking your phone or accessing secure networks just by thinking. It might sound like science fiction, but **brainwave authentication**, or **EEG biometrics (Electroencephalogram)**, is being explored as a futuristic yet viable method of identity verification.

How It Works:

- EEG sensors (via wearable headbands or neural implants) detect brainwave patterns generated by cognitive responses to specific stimuli (images, sounds, thoughts).

- These patterns, influenced by neural pathways, are unique to each individual—even identical twins have different brainwaves.

- Some systems use **pass-thoughts**, where users think of a specific memory or image as a mental password.

Advantages:

- **Highly secure** – difficult to replicate or steal.

- Immune to visual spoofing or fingerprint lifting.

- Useful for people with disabilities who can't use traditional biometrics.

Challenges:

- EEG devices are still bulky and expensive.

- Brainwave patterns can vary due to fatigue, mood, or external noise.

- Raises profound **ethical and psychological concerns** about mind-reading and mental privacy.

---

3. Quantum Cryptography: Unbreakable Digital Locks

Biometric systems are only as secure as the data that supports them. Spoofing often targets **stored biometric templates**, which, once stolen, cannot be replaced. Enter **Quantum Cryptography**, a field that promises *unbreakable data transmission and storage* using the laws of quantum mechanics.

What is It?

- Based on **quantum key distribution (QKD)**, which ensures that any interception attempt will alter the key itself, thus alerting both sender and receiver.

- Used to transmit biometric data securely without the risk of duplication or tampering.

Use Cases in Biometrics:

- Protecting **biometric templates** in transit and storage.

- Securing **multimodal systems** where various biometric data are combined.

- Implementing **post-quantum biometric authentication** for government and military-grade access control.

Advantages:

- **Theoretically unhackable** by classical or quantum computers.

- Prevents man-in-the-middle and replay attacks.

- Future-proof against quantum computing threats.

Challenges:

- Still in **experimental or niche deployment**.

- Requires expensive hardware and **quantum-safe infrastructure**.

- Adoption limited to high-security sectors—so far.

---

4. Zero Trust Architecture (ZTA): Never Trust, Always Verify

Zero Trust is not a biometric system per se, but a **security philosophy** that fundamentally reshapes how we approach authentication and access. In a **Zero Trust Architecture**, no one—inside or outside the network—is trusted by default.

Key Principles:

- **Continuous verification** of identity, context, and device health.

- **Least-privilege access**—users get only what they need, nothing more.

- **Microsegmentation** of networks to isolate threats.

- Constant monitoring for anomalies.

Role of Biometrics in ZTA:

- Biometrics serve as one of many factors in **adaptive authentication**.

- Behavioral biometrics can monitor session integrity over time.

- Liveness detection becomes essential in preventing identity hijack during sessions.

Advantages:

- Prevents **lateral movement** of threats within a network.

- Detects and stops compromised biometrics through real-time analytics.

- Reduces reliance on perimeter-based defense (which biometrics alone can't secure).

Challenges:

- Requires **cultural shift** and investment in infrastructure.

- Integration with legacy systems can be difficult.

- May increase friction if not implemented thoughtfully.

Looking Ahead: A Hybrid Future

The future of biometric security lies not in a silver bullet, but in **synergy**. Expect to see:

- **Multimodal systems** combining face, voice, behavior, and contextual data.

- **Decentralized biometric IDs** stored on personal devices, not central databases.

- **AI-driven anomaly detection** to sniff out spoofing attempts before they escalate.

- **User-controlled privacy**, where biometric data is cryptographically sealed and locally stored.

The mantra going forward is clear: **Trust no single method. Verify continuously. Adapt intelligently.**

Conclusion: The Next Frontier of Trust

As attackers grow smarter, security systems must grow wiser. The evolution of biometric security will be shaped not only by technological progress but by **ethical foresight, privacy consciousness**, and **user-centric design**.

The human body might be the password of the future, but it must be protected by a fortress built with innovation, insight, and integrity.

11. Conclusion

Biometric authentication has reshaped how we think about security. It offers a seamless blend of convenience and sophistication, enabling users to access devices, facilities, and services using nothing more than their unique physical or behavioral traits. Whether it's a fingerprint unlocking a smartphone, facial recognition granting access to secure buildings, or iris scans verifying identity at international borders, biometrics have quickly become integrated into our daily lives.

Yet, as with any powerful technology, biometrics are not immune to misuse and exploitation.

The Allure and the Achilles' Heel

The central appeal of biometric systems lies in their perceived infallibility. After all, no two people (supposedly) share the same fingerprints, irises, or voiceprints. Unlike traditional security systems that rely on something you know (like a password) or something you have (like a security token), biometrics are based on something you *are*. This inherent uniqueness fosters a false sense of security, leading individuals and organizations to adopt these technologies with minimal skepticism or layered protection.

But herein lies the flaw: **biometric traits can be stolen, copied, or spoofed**, often with alarming ease. Once compromised, a biometric cannot be "changed" or "reset" like a password. Your fingerprints, facial structure, and voice remain the same for life, making spoofing a long-term threat.

88

Spoofing: A Growing and Evolving Threat

The rise of biometric spoofing is not hypothetical—it's a very real and evolving challenge. Researchers, ethical hackers, and even malicious actors have repeatedly demonstrated the vulnerability of these systems. From printing fingerprints using gelatin or 3D molds to using deepfake videos and AI-synthesized voices, spoofing techniques are growing more sophisticated and accessible.

The democratization of artificial intelligence has only accelerated this threat. AI-generated biometric data—voice, face, even gait—can now be produced with chilling accuracy. Spoofing no longer requires a lab or expensive equipment; in some cases, all it takes is a high-resolution photo or a few seconds of voice recording found on social media.

The Role of Liveness Detection and AI Defenses

To combat this, developers have turned to **liveness detection** and AI-based anti-spoofing algorithms. These technologies aim to ensure that the biometric trait presented is from a live person and not a replica. They measure everything from micro-expressions and pupil dilation to skin texture and blood flow. AI tools, trained on massive datasets, learn to differentiate real traits from forgeries.

However, the cat-and-mouse game continues. As anti-spoofing defenses improve, so too do the tools of the attackers. Deepfake technology evolves to bypass facial liveness tests. Voice cloning becomes so realistic that even nuanced emotional cues are mimicked. The line between authentic and artificial blurs dangerously.

Layered Security: The New Imperative

In this landscape, relying solely on biometrics is no longer prudent. **Layered security**—or multi-factor authentication (MFA)—must become the norm. Combining biometrics with something you know (PIN, password) or something you have (a device or token) dramatically increases the difficulty of a successful spoofing attack.

Organizations must also implement **risk-based authentication**, adapting the level of scrutiny depending on the context of the access attempt. Logging in from a new location? Using a different device? Performing a high-risk transaction? These should trigger additional verification steps.

Equally important is the concept of **continuous authentication**—where a system constantly verifies the user's identity through behavioral biometrics and activity patterns, rather than relying on a one-time check.

Privacy and Ethical Considerations

Beyond security, biometric systems pose serious privacy and ethical questions. When your biometric data is collected— often passively and without explicit consent—it can be stored, analyzed, and even sold. Massive biometric databases maintained by governments and corporations are prime targets for cyberattacks. And once breached, the damage is irreversible.

Ethical deployment of biometrics must include transparency, user consent, strict data governance, and compliance with privacy regulations like the GDPR and CCPA. The push for innovation must not come at the expense of civil liberties or personal autonomy.

A Call for Awareness and Caution

Ultimately, the strength of any security system lies not just in its technology, but in the **awareness of its users and administrators**. The myth of biometric invincibility must be dispelled. Biometric spoofing is not science fiction—it is science fact.

As we embrace convenience, we must do so with our eyes open. The tools we use to protect ourselves can also be turned against us. Vigilance, education, and continuous improvement are vital.

Final Thoughts

In a world where we can now unlock our phones with a glance and start our cars with a touch, it is easy to be lulled into complacency. Biometrics, while powerful, are just one piece of the security puzzle. They must be implemented with foresight, defended with cutting-edge tools, and accompanied by responsible policies.

Let us remember: even the most unique traits of the human body—our fingerprints, voices, and faces—can be mimicked, duplicated, and deceived. In the wrong hands, the very features that make us who we are can become the key to our undoing.

Security is not about perfect systems—it's about resilient systems. And resilience begins with understanding the threats.

Bibliography

1. **Handbook of Biometric Anti-Spoofing** by Sébastien Marcel, Mark S. Nixon, and Julian Fierrez

2. **Introduction to Biometrics** by Anil K. Jain, Arun Ross, and Karthik Nandakumar

3. **Biometric Systems: Technology, Design and Performance Evaluation** by James L. Wayman et al.

4. **Deepfakes: The Coming Infocalypse** by Nina Schick

5. **Security Engineering: A Guide to Building Dependable Distributed Systems** by Ross Anderson

6. **Cybersecurity and Cyberwar: What Everyone Needs to Know** by P.W. Singer and Allan Friedman

7. **Hacking the Human: Social Engineering Techniques and Security Countermeasures** by Ian Mann

8. **Privacy in the Age of Big Data** by Theresa Payton and Ted Claypoole

9. **The Master Algorithm** by Pedro Domingos

Acknowledgments

This book has been a journey through the intricate world of biometric technology, and it would not have been possible without the support, encouragement, and insights of many individuals and organizations.

First and foremost, I would like to express my sincere gratitude to the dedicated researchers, cybersecurity professionals, and ethical hackers whose work continues to shine a light on the vulnerabilities and strengths of biometric systems. Your relentless pursuit of truth and security laid the foundation upon which this book stands.

To the pioneers in biometric science and the countless developers behind the technologies we explore and rely on daily—thank you for pushing the boundaries of innovation and for creating the systems that inspired this exploration.

A special thank you to the academic and open-source communities that provide invaluable resources, papers, and discussions on biometric spoofing and countermeasures online. Your openness and dedication to knowledge-sharing made this work infinitely richer.

Lastly, to the readers—those curious minds who seek to understand, question, and improve the technologies shaping our future—this book is for you. May it empower you with knowledge and inspire a safer, more secure digital world.

With appreciation,
Zahid Ameer

Disclaimer

This book, *Biometric Spoofing: Unmasking the Illusion of Security*, is intended for educational and informational purposes only. While it explores various techniques and concepts related to biometric spoofing and security vulnerabilities, the content is not intended to promote, encourage, or support any form of illegal or unethical activity.

The author and publisher do not assume responsibility for any misuse of the information provided in this book. Readers are advised to use the knowledge shared herein to enhance awareness, improve cybersecurity practices, and foster responsible innovation in the field of biometric authentication.

All opinions expressed are those of the author and do not reflect the views of any organizations, institutions, or entities mentioned. Readers should consult qualified professionals for legal or technical advice related to biometric security or cybersecurity implementations.

Use this knowledge wisely—ethical responsibility and respect for privacy should always guide your actions.

About me

I am Zahid Ameer, hailing from the vibrant country of India. As an author, ghostwriter, bibliophile, online affiliate marketer, blogger, YouTuber, graphic designer, and animal lover, I have woven my passions into a unique tapestry that defines my life's work.

Born and raised in India, I have always possessed a deep love for literature. With an insatiable appetite for books, I have amassed an impressive collection of around 1,600 titles, predominantly in English. My passion for reading brings me immense joy and serves as a source of inspiration for my writing endeavors.

I have compiled an impressive portfolio of written works as an author and ghostwriter. With a captivating writing style and an innate ability to craft engaging narratives, I bring my stories to life, captivating readers from all walks of life. My wide range of interests and experiences contribute to the richness of my writing, allowing me to connect with my audience on a heartfelt level effortlessly.

Beyond my literary pursuits, I have also established a strong presence on various digital platforms. I utilize my YouTube channel and blog to raise awareness about all types of knowledge and to share heartwarming stories of animals. Using my platform to shed light on important issues, I strive to create a world where humans and animals can coexist harmoniously.

In addition to my work as an author, I have also dabbled in the world of affiliate marketing. With my webpreneur spirit, I have ventured into online marketing, leveraging my knowledge and skills to promote products and services that align with my values.

However, my most cherished role is that of a father. Family is at the core of my being, and everything I do is centered around creating a better future for my loved ones. My dedication to my family is evident in my passion for personal growth and my relentless pursuit of success. Through my various endeavors, I strive to set an example of perseverance and ambition for my children, inspiring them to chase their dreams unapologetically.

In a world where specialization often dominates, I defy convention by embracing multiple passions and excelling in diverse fields. My love for books, animals, and family has become the driving force behind my achievements. By the grace of Almighty God, my unique blend of characteristics has allowed me to leave an indelible mark on the world, enriching the lives of those I encounter along the way.

To your grand success in life,

Zahid Ameer

Biometric Spoofing

Versatile Indie Author
<u>Follow me on X</u>